YOGA

✳ A practical, step-by-step guide to yoga postures ✳

Published by Abbeydale Press
An imprint of Bookmart Ltd
Registered number 2372865
Trading as Bookmart Ltd
Desford Road
Enderby
Leicester LE19 4AD

Produced for Bookmart by BodyBooks, a division of Mitchell Lewis Editions Ltd
Email:info@mitchell-lewis.com

ISBN 1 86147 102 5

Printed in Singapore

Editorial Director	Sarah Constable
Art Director	Joyce Mason
Editor	Carey Denton
Photographer	Graham Atkins Hughes
Hair and Make-up	Liberty Shaw
Yoga postures demonstated by	Jean Hall, Louise Taylor and Alan Kelly
Index	Susan Bosanko

PUBLISHER'S NOTE

Before following any advice or practice suggested in this book, it
is recommended that you consult the doctor as to its suitability,
especially if you suffer from any health problems or special
conditions. The publishers, the author and the photographers
cannot accept responsibility for any injuries or damage incurred
as a result of following the exercises in this book, or of using
any of the therapeutic methods described or mentioned here.

YOGA

* A practical, step-by-step guide to yoga postures *

Jean Hall

ABBEYDALE PRESS

contents

CHAPTER **3** spirit *Closing Your Practice* *62*

CHAPTER **4** living yoga *Yoga Sequences* *70*

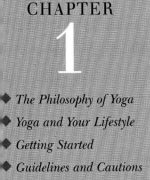

mind

Understanding Yoga

Yoga is the world's oldest system of self-development and encompasses mind, body and spirit. There are many forms, styles and practices of yoga, but they all share the same aim, that of connecting and uniting with the divine.

Hatha yoga is the most popular yoga practised in the West and is the physical component, the postures and breathing exercises, of a broader path called Raja yoga, which is often described as the royal path of the body and mind.

The term 'yoga' originates from the Sanskrit root *yuj* meaning to yoke, unite, join together as one. Hatha translates as sun, *ha*, and moon, *tha*, and so Hatha yoga literally means sun and moon joining together as one. The solar and lunar energies represent the opposing elements of nature and the opposing qualities within humanity, such as heaven and earth, male and female, day and night, intellect and emotion, hot and cold, dry and moist, weight and weightlessness, active and passive, fullness and emptiness.

Through the practice of Hatha yoga we follow clear steps which help to integrate and harmonize these aspects of ourselves, bringing about balance, health and energy in our mind, body and spirit.

The Philosophy of Yoga

Yoga is one of the six fundamental systems of Indian philosophical thought and has its origin in the *Vedas*, an ancient collection of Sanskrit sacred hymns and poems, philosophical suppositions, ancient lore and ritualistic traditions which are believed to be over three and a half thousand years old. Ecstatics are referred to in these texts and they are believed to be the forerunners of the earliest yogis.

The ancient yogis – followers of yoga – were seekers of truth, exploring the essential nature of humanity, and learning how to live in harmony with the self and their surroundings.

They believed the physical body to be a container housing the soul, which they understood to be an individual's truest identity. In yoga philosophy the mind is considered the driving force, and emotion and intelligence motivate the body into action. Inspired by the landscape, elements, animals, birds and plants the yogis

Brahma, the Hindu creator of the universe, holds a page of the Vedas – *a sacred Sanskrit manuscript that records the earliest reference to yoga.*

developed movements and postures for physical health, and breathing and meditation practices to liberate the mind allowing the individual to connect with the higher self.

Different paths of yoga practice are outlined in the *Bhagavad Gita* (Song of The Lord), one of the greatest Hindu scriptures, which is contained within the Sanskrit epic the *Mahabharata*. The *Bhagavad Gita* is a dialogue between the young warrior prince, Arjuna and the Hindu Lord Krishna in which the ageless issues of ethical living, moral dilemmas, selflessness and steadiness of the mind are raised. Krishna outlines three paths to God: Jnana yoga – the path of knowledge and wisdom; Bhakti yoga – the path of devotion and love; and Karma yoga – the path of selfless service and action. Each path serves to accommodate different personalities or character temperaments, but share the same aims of realizing our potential, uniting with our true nature and bringing about happiness, compassion and health.

The seven chakras, which literally mean 'wheels', are housed along the spine, or the subtle pathway of the spine called the sushumna.

THE CHAKRA SYSTEM

In yoga philosophy, it is thought that the body contains seven primary centres of life energy or prana. *These are called* chakras *and, on a physical level, they correspond to key nerve centres or plexuses in the body. Yoga practice awakens the* chakras, *releasing energy and spiritually raising the consciousness from the lower to the higher self. This can take years – or more likely a lifetime!*

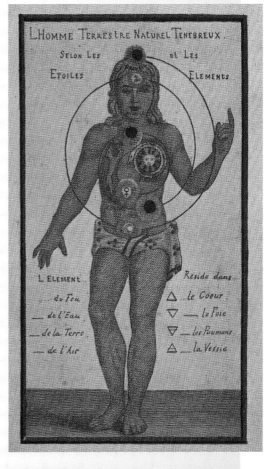

First chakra

Muladhara chakra is the source of all primal energy and is located at the base of the spine. Its element is earth and its symbol is a lotus flower with four deep red petals.

Second chakra

Swadhisthana chakra is the centre of desire and deep-rooted instincts. Found three fingers' width below the navel, it is depicted as a crimson lotus with six petals and its element is water.

Third chakra

Manipura chakra is the seat of power, energy and assertiveness. It corresponds to the solar plexus and is depicted as a bright yellow lotus with 10 petals and its element is fire.

Fourth chakra

Anahata chakra is the centre of compassion, tolerance and love. Situated at the level of the heart it is symbolized by a smoky blue lotus with 12 petals. Its element is air.

Fifth chakra

Vishuddha chakra is the centre of purity concerned with right understanding. It is located at the throat. Depicted as a violet lotus with 16 petals, its element is ether.

Sixth chakra

Ajna chakra is the centre of wisdom, intuition and balance. Depicted as a silver lotus with two petals representing moon and sun energy, its element is space and its physical place is between the eyebrows.

Seventh chakra

Sahasrara chakra is the abode of our highest consciousness, located at the crown of the head. It is depicted by a lotus of a thousand glowing petals. It is said, when energy flows to this chakra enlightenment is attained.

The Eight Limbs of Yoga

The eight limbs of yoga provide a clear and profound pathway that guides us through the physical, mental and spiritual practices that lead towards enlightenment, or *samadhi*.

The Yoga Sutras *are considered the most significant text on Raja yoga, which is a branch of the yoga tree that incorporates spiritual and physical practices. (The physical practice, the poses and breathing, is called Hatha yoga.) The* Yoga Sutras *provide the aspiring yogi with a thread, or* sutra, *to follow through each stage of the yoga journey. Very little is known about the author, Patanjali, except that he is believed to have written this text during the first or second century CE. The* Yoga Sutras *contain four chapters, each one denoting a*

1 ABSTENTIONS

The five *Yamas* which clear negativity from the body and heart.

Ahimsa: compassion and non-violence in our behaviour to all sentient beings. Be kind.

Satya: truthfulness in thought, word and deed. Be honest and kind.

Asteya: do not steal. Be generous.

Brahmacharya: self-restraint. Be moderate in all things.

Aparigraha: non-possessiveness and non-greed. Be sharing.

2 OBSERVANCES

The five *Niyamas* for our personal discipline.

Shauca: cleanliness, keeping ourselves and our environment clean and fresh.

Samtosha: contentment and acceptance of reality. Allowing ourselves to appreciate and be happy with what we have and who we are, even as we strive for self-improvement.

Tapas: discipline in order to grow, develop and care for ourselves and others.

Svadhyaya: study of the self. Being reflective and introspective helps us get to know our deeper nature, creating clarity in our lives.

Ishvarapranidhana: devotion. Living with constant awareness of the divine presence.

3 YOGA POSTURES

Yogasanas

The practice of yoga postures helps us to build confidence in ourselves as well as developing physical health.

different stage, level and approach to yoga. The first chapter explains yoga and deals with the fluctuations of the mind and the obstacles it creates for the yoga practitioner. The second chapter outlines the eight limbs of yoga, detailed here. The third chapter discusses the potential of the mind and extrasensory awareness that can be gained through the mastery of yoga. The fourth chapter deals with the final journey of the soul towards release and liberation. Written many centuries ago, the Sutras *are still a trusted guide to yoga practice.*

4 BREATH REGULATION

Pranayama

Breath is life. By regulating our breath we can change our breathing patterns and consequently our patterns of being, opening ourselves up to boundless possibilities.

5 SENSE WITHDRAWAL

Pratyahara

By looking inwards and dropping our ties and over-attachment to the stimulants and activities of the outside world, we can begin to connect with our inner self and nature. Certain *yogasanas* and *pranayama* evoke *pratyahara*.

6 CONCENTRATION

Dharana

This develops attention span, mental alertness and awareness so we can focus on one matter, object, sensation or thought at a time. Exercises in *dharana* include looking at an object, such as a candle flame, or being completely attentive to the sound and feeling of your breath.

7 MEDITATION

Dhyana

Through the practice of concentration, *dharana*, meditation becomes possible by bringing us into deep connection with the object of our attention, so that everything else ceases to exist, creating oneness and total awareness.

8 ENLIGHTENMENT

Samadhi

Samadhi means to merge into oneness. In enlightenment we merge not just with our object of meditation, but with all universal consciousness, liberating ourselves from the struggle of duality and separateness of us and them, him and her, fair and unfair: because we are all here in the essence of all things.

Yoga and Your Lifestyle

Yoga has been practised for thousands of years, and is as relevant today as it ever was. Although it helps to develop beautiful fit bodies, yoga was originally practised by seekers of truth and self-knowledge. Embracing yoga can enrich our lives on many levels, helping us find inner calm in a fast and stressful world, whilst promoting total body health.

PHYSICAL BENEFITS OF YOGA

The benefits of yoga are multi-faceted. Yoga is a journey of the body, mind and spirit. Through the practice of yoga postures the body becomes fit, toned, supple and agile. Internal organs are gently massaged and bodily processes stimulated.

The mind becomes clear and the nervous system soothed through regulated breathing, *pranayama*. Respiration is improved, generating vitality.

Yoga is also a healing system, so for those who have suffered injury or trauma it is a path to recovery. Bones realign, muscles unlock, physical and emotional tensions are released and new energy begins to flow through our bodies.

EMOTIONAL WELL-BEING

As we begin to feel energized with our fitter bodies, this can positively affect our mental and emotional well-being, allowing us to feel at ease and more complete in our-selves. This can have a knock-on

THE YOGA DIET

Yoga practitioners believe that food contains a combination of three primal qualities known as gunas. *These are pure or* sattva, *inert or* tamas, *and active or* rajas. Gunas *are qualities which exist together and are present at all times in all things, not just food.*

FOOD GROUPS

SATTVIC FOODS

Pure, unprocessed, simple and fresh. These foods are preservative free (organic), non-addictive and non-harming. They create balance, clarity and vitality on a mental, physical and spiritual level as they are clean foods free of mood-altering chemicals.

RAJASIC FOODS

These are spicy, pungent, bitter and hot foods. They over-stimulate the body and mind and can cause restlessness, anxiety and stress. Eating quickly is also considered *rajasic*.

TAMASIC FOODS

Old, stale, aged, fermented, cold and dry. These foods drain the body's energy, causing fatigue and dulling of the mind. (Meat and caffeine are both *rajasic* and *tamasic* as they initially stimulate the body then cause energy levels to drop.)

Ideally the main part of our diet needs to be made up of sattvic *foods, pure foods in their natural state – unprocessed and preferably organic – to bring our minds and bodies into a balanced and healthy state of being.*

SOURCES

Fresh vegetables and salads.

Fresh fruit and juices, and dried fruit.

Pulses such as beans and lentils.

Wholemeal cereals and bread,

Milk, butter and cheese.

Nuts, seeds and sprouted seeds.

Herbs, herb teas, honey and water.

Meats, fish and eggs.

Peppers and salt.

Strong spices like chillies.

Tea, coffee and other caffeine-laden foods like chocolate and cola.

Refined sugar.

Meats.

Mushrooms, because they grow in the dark.

Onions and garlic.

Tobacco and alcohol.

Fermented vinegar.

Coffee and tea.

effect within our relationships and ways of dealing with life and its challenges. We begin to feel balanced and centred, not depending on others to validate us. We can trust ourselves and our own worth. We are clearer-thinking, cooler-headed, kinder-hearted. In this way yoga can reach beyond ourselves and touch others.

THE WIDER PICTURE

The practice of yoga postures is just one aspect of yoga. To gain the full benefits we need to take care of the other basics: diet, sleep, rest and play.

Yoga promotes a vegetarian diet based on natural, unprocessed foods. These foods come from the soil and are believed to carry unadulterated life force. We are encouraged to eat slowly and not to overload our systems.

The yoga practitioner may notice a change in tastes. Perhaps eating less, or wanting to eat differently, or not wanting to drink so much alcohol or giving up smoking. We can listen to and trust these messages from our bodies: eat when we feel hungry, don't if we don't! When we feel tired, sleep or at least rest. And play – it is important to kick back, lighten up and have fun.

Yoga is a personal journey: each one of us must decide how deeply we wish to bring it into our lives. Yoga can remain a small part, or we can embrace the lifestyle and follow the teachings more fully.

Getting Started

I t is always advisable to learn yoga with a qualified teacher. A beginners' class will teach you the foundations of the basic postures. Look for a class which isn't crowded – between 10-16 students – as this will allow the teacher to get to know each student, recognize special needs and give individual attention. The class also needs to be at a convenient time and venue, otherwise it becomes a stressful chore to get there, and ends up being counter-productive.

Teachers vary enormously in their styles of teaching, so look for one you feel comfortable with, who resonates well with you, and gives good clear instructions and correction both verbally and physically. Finding the right teacher may take time, so don't give up. The saying goes, "when the student is ready the teacher will appear!".

The wonderful thing about yoga is that it can be practised virtually anywhere. All you need is a little clear space, a non-slip surface and yourself. When practising yoga at home create a conducive environment: light candles, burn incense, lie a yoga mat out, shut the door, open the window and begin!

Individual practice is an important aspect of yoga. Even when you are going to regular classes take time to practise on your own. This allows you to have a time of contemplation, and move in and out of the postures at your own pace and rhythm.

There are many different schools of yoga; make sure you pick a class that is suited to you and a teacher who can give you individual attention.

STYLES OF HATHA YOGA

There are many different approaches to Hatha yoga, each one as valid as the next. The postures are their common ground, but the emphasis in teaching them is their diversity. For example one style may focus in particular on the alignment of the body in the yoga poses, whilst another may highlight the spiritual aspects. It is important to choose the style which you feel most interested in and most suited to.

Iyengar Alignment and in-depth understanding of the body in the yoga postures is central, and therefore this style is suitable for all levels. Moderated postures are taught with the use of props which can be very beneficial for those with injuries and physical restrictions. BKS Iyengar is perhaps the world's most famous yoga teacher.

Sivananda teaches the five basic principles of proper relaxation, proper exercise, proper breathing, proper diet and positive thinking with meditation. Classes focus on 12 basic postures, relaxation, breathing and can include chanting and spiritual teachings. Suitable for all levels of fitness. Swami Sivananda is the pioneer of this approach.

Viniyoga is taught in small groups and on a one-to-one basis, so it is ideal for all. Its aim to is to develop a personal approach to yoga and also includes therapeutic, philosophical and spiritual teachings. Desikachar, who is the son of the late, great yoga teacher Krishnamacharya, developed this school of thought.

Astanga Vinyasa yoga A dynamic flow of a set sequence of postures. Classes are either led by a teacher who talks the students through the sequence or are self-practise, where the students know the series of postures already and practise them at their own pace with the teacher making physical corrections. Astanga is

physically demanding so is best suited to those who are in good health. Pattabhi Jois is the founder of this style.

Bikram yoga For those who like to sweat! These classes are taught in rooms which are heated to more than 100°F/38°C, so they are really only for those with a good level of fitness. Bikram Choudury developed this system of yoga.

A yoga holiday or retreat allows you to practise without distractions in beautiful, even exotic surroundings. Eat well, exercise well and recharge your batteries.

Guidelines and Cautions

Comfortable clothing, that won't restrict your movements or get in the way as you practise the postures, is perfect for yoga.

The yoga poses, breathing and meditation practices presented in this book introduce the reader to the core elements of Hatha yoga. However, a book cannot replace a qualified teacher and to progress in yoga you will need to join a suitable class. Read through the instructions of each pose before practising it and remember to listen to your body: if you feel any strain or discomfort, you have gone too far. Each pose is described under its heading as a soft, medium or strong pose to give you some guidance about which poses are suitable for you.

GOLDEN RULES

■ **Always practise** with patience, care and attention.

■ **Never practise on a full stomach** and always allow a minimum of two hours after food before you begin.

■ **Drink water before and after your practice,** but not during, as this will interrupt your flow and cool your internal heat, which is created during yoga to burn off toxins.

■ **Yoga is always practised barefoot** as this enhances awareness of the feet and a sense of grounding.

■ **Practise in a space that is clean and warm.** Try to keep a clear uncluttered small space for yoga as it will help you focus and stop you becoming side-tracked. Warmth is also important. Your muscles will become more supple and respond more effectively when practising in a warm room.

Frequent practice is the key to progress with yoga. Small sessions of individual practice three or four times a week are more helpful than a longer session less frequently.

■ **Never hold your breath in postures,** always focus on breathing smoothly, softly and steadily through your nose.

■ **Wear soft comfortable clothing**, tight clothing can restrict your movements, whilst baggy clothing will get in the way.

■ **Regular practice** is the key to progress and gaining the benefits of yoga. Short regular practice sessions carry more benefit than the occasional blitz! Aim at first to practise for 20-30 minutes three or four times a week and then gradually increase each session to 60-90 minutes.

■ **To begin with,** stay in each posture for five breaths, then as you build up stamina and flexibility you may want to stay in the pose for longer.

■ **Try one of the yoga sequences** in Living Yoga (pages 70-77). Once you have become familiar with the *asanas* and sequences you can begin to develop your own practice and create your own routine of poses.

■ **Start with postures** you feel comfortable with and then gradually progress on to more challenging ones.

■ **If you have a medical condition, or any concerns about your health, check with your doctor first that yoga is suitable for you.**

YOGA PROPS

Props are helpful for beginners, for those working with restricted movement and tight muscles, and for remedial work after an injury.

a *Yoga practice mats:* a mat provides a slightly padded, non-slip surface, essential for yoga work.

b *Blocks:* sit on blocks to lift the pelvis up and lengthen and support the spine. Also helpful for a stiff back or tight hamstring.

c *Bolster:* use a bolster to lean over in seated bends, or to relax back on.

d *Sandbag:* helps you deepen your postures by adding weight. *Eyebag (front):* use to block out light as a relaxation aid.

e *Strap:* if you lack flexibility, a strap will help you reach towards another part of your body without straining.

17

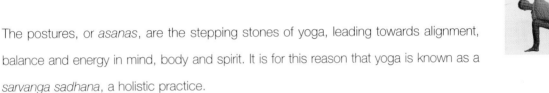

Yoga Postures

The postures, or *asanas*, are the stepping stones of yoga, leading towards alignment, balance and energy in mind, body and spirit. It is for this reason that yoga is known as a *sarvanga sadhana*, a holistic practice.

Each group of postures creates physical and mental benefits. The standing poses develop a balance between strength and flexibility. They bring vitality and power to the feet, legs and pelvis, whilst toning and invigorating the whole body.

Sitting poses have a soothing effect on both body and mind. They give the legs respite from carrying the weight of the body and help to revive and release tightness in the leg muscles, calm the nervous system and remove tension from the brain.

Twists are essential for spinal health as they stimulate the spinal nerves and create suppleness in the back muscles. They also have powerful detoxifying benefits as they literally wring the toxins out of the internal organs. Back bends also encourage flexibility as well as improving circulation and generating energy and freshness in body and mind. Inverted poses allow us to put our feet up which in essence rejuvenates, replenishes and revitalizes the complete bodily system.

Preparing to Practise

Try starting each yoga session by sitting quietly in Happy Pose (page 38) or adopting Child's Pose (page 64), for a few minutes, listening to your breath, consciously relaxing the mind and body. This will help you unwind, tune into your energy and focus your mind for your practice.

When practising yoga it is important to work gently but deeply, consciously focusing on the subtle sensations of each of the *asanas* (see Practice Tips).

It is important never to force or pull your body into a posture, instead release and gently stretch your body into the pose. Never hold the body rigid; always gently explore each pose by allowing the body to open and release deeper and deeper into the stillness and alignment of the *asana*.

Bring your mind to focus on the yoga practice ahead by sitting in Happy Pose (page 38) and breathing deeply, gently and steadily in and out of your nose. Quieten your mind and listen to your breath.

PRACTICE TIPS
As you start each yoga session be sure to move slowly, taking about 5-10 breaths in each pose before moving on to the next one.

Happy Pose (page 38)

Yoga Sealing Pose
(page 64)

These yoga postures will gently limber up and prepare your body for practice. Read through the instructions on the pages indicated before beginning. Only do Step 1 and 2 of the Knee Hug Pose (page 41) and remember to hug each leg into the body in turn.

Child's Pose (page 64)

*Standing Forward
Bend Pose* (page 30)

Knee Hug Pose
(page 41)

Mountain Pose
Tadasana ◆ soft pose

Mountain Pose is the most important posture as it lays the foundations for all the other standing poses. It is the first step in learning the *asanas* and the starting position for many of the other standing poses.

Tadasana teaches us correct posture and alignment as we become centred in our bodies and grounded through our feet. It promotes balance, tone and an ability to be still and strong like a mountain.

GENTLER VARIATION

If standing with your feet together is uncomfortable or you find it difficult to balance, try standing with your feet slightly apart. Make sure they are directly in line under your hips.

PRACTICE TIPS

As you stand in Mountain Pose take time to feel your feet sink into the ground and breathe length into your spine.

1 **Starting position** Stand with your feet together. Centre your weight evenly over both legs and feel the soles of your feet opening into the floor. Lengthen your spine out of your hips and let your tailbone sink. Draw up your kneecaps, thighs and lower abdomen. Feel your chest opening as your arms and fingers gently extend towards the floor.

2 **Relax your shoulders,** allowing your shoulder-blades to slide down. Lengthen the back of your neck and soften your chin, bringing it down slightly. Soften your gaze keeping your eyes relaxed and breathe smoothly in the pose for 10-20 breaths.

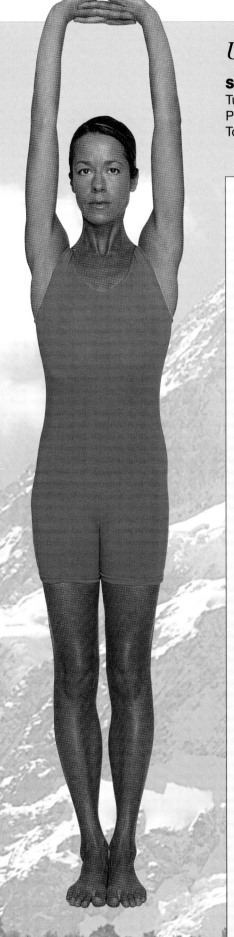

Upward Mountain Pose

Stand in Mountain Pose, bring your palms together and interlace your fingers. Turn your palms out and stretch your arms up, keeping your shoulders drawn down. Push your palms up and press your feet down and take 5-10 breaths. To come out of the pose, exhale and lower your arms.

Awakening the Feet

Our feet are of great significance and their importance is often overlooked. They carry us through life, so we need to look after them well and stand on them kindly! Standing poses give us the ideal opportunity to focus on correct stance and to check that we are not misusing our feet. If the feet are misaligned, the rest of the body will be too.

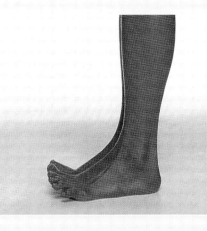 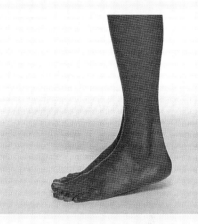

1 **To awaken your feet** rock back on your heels and lift the balls of your feet off the floor, spreading your toes out and away from one another.

2 **Roll the ball and toes** back down on to the ground lifting your heels up. Repeat 2-3 times, then settle your weight evenly on your heels and toes.

Standing Correctly – Do's and Don'ts

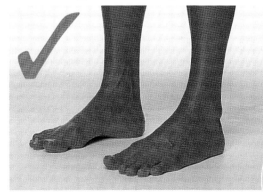

Don't allow your weight to drop on to the inner edges of your feet as this will cause your arches to collapse and cause misalignment of your whole leg.

Extend your weight through your heels, your big toe joints and especially the outer edges of your feet to develop and maintain a lift of the arches. Spread your toes and open the soles of your feet downwards.

The Sun Salutation

Surya Namaskar ◆◆ medium pose

The Sun Salutation is an ancient Indian practice that draws sunlight and energy into the body and mind, awakening our entire being. It is traditionally practised at the break of dawn, just before the sun rises, to welcome in the new day.

It is a fluid and graceful sequence that links 12 postures together, harmonizing the movement of your body with the motion of your breath. The Sun Salutation warms the muscles and gently awakens the body preparing it for the yoga practice that follows. As you softly move through this sequence, keep listening to your breath and allow it to become steady and rhythmical. Remember to breathe through the nose and let your inhalation and exhalation carry you into each pose.

PRACTICE TIPS

When you are first learning this sequence, take a few breaths in each posture to familiarize yourself with the feel, alignment and form of each one. Gradually develop a flow of movement with the flow of your breath.

1 **Mountain Pose** (page 22). Stand quietly in this pose.

12 **Exhale as you lower your arms** to your sides and return quietly to Mountain Pose.

11 **Inhale and lift your body,** raising your arms up sideways above your head with the palms together. Look up.

10 **Exhale as you step your right foot forward.** Place your feet together with the legs straight, and release your body down over your legs with your hands on your ankles or the floor.

9 **Inhale and step your left foot foward** in between your hands, lift your chest and rest your right knee on the floor.

2 **Inhale and stretch** your arms up with the palms together. Look up to your hands.

3 **Exhale and fold your body** forward over the legs, hinging at the hips, relax your neck and place your hands at the side of your feet or on your ankles if your cannot reach the floor.

4 **Inhale and extend your right leg back,** toes tucked under, and stretch your spine forward. Let your right knee rest on the floor and look forwards.

5 **Retain the breath** and draw your left leg back, supporting your weight evenly on your hands and toes.

6 **Exhale and bend your elbows in** towards your waist and lower your knees and chest to the floor. Keep your hips lifted and do not drop your belly on to the ground.

7 **Inhale, lengthen your spine,** straighten your arms and lift your chest and face skywards. At the same time, lower your hips and stretch your legs and feet back, with the tops of your feet flat on the floor. Draw your shoulders down.

8 **Exhale, curl your toes under** and lift your hips up and back. Press your heels down and bring your chin towards your chest.

Triangle Pose

Trikonasana ◆ soft pose

Triangle Pose helps to create stability and balance in the body, bringing strength and alignment to the feet, ankles, legs, hips and spine. The back lengthens and the chest opens, helping to relieve backache and release tension from the neck and shoulders.

1 Starting position From Mountain Pose step your feet about 1.2m (4ft) apart, with feet parallel and toes pointing forwards. Stretch your arms out at shoulder level and draw your shoulder-blades down. Lengthen your spine and broaden your back.

PRACTICE TIPS

Develop strength and tone in your legs by drawing your arches, knees and thigh muscles up when in the full pose. Keep your chest and arms open and shoulders soft.

2 Turn the toes and the ball of your left foot inward by 10-15°. Rotate your right leg out from the top of your thigh by 90°, so that your inner thigh draws forwards and your right toes, knee and thigh all face to the right. Place your right heel in line with your left arch. Gently lift your lower abdomen.

3 Exhale as you lengthen and extend your body to the right side. Place your right hand lightly on your shin, ankle or the ground depending on how deep you are able to reach over (see Gentler Variation). Stretch your left arm up with the palm facing forwards and the hand in line with your left shoulder.

GENTLER VARIATION

Keep your hand on the ankle or shin, if taking the hand lower causes your body to collapse or tilts you forward. Concentrate on learning to extend your body sideways.

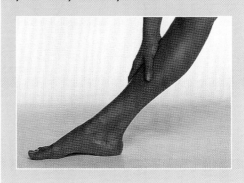

4 Take about 5-10 breaths in the pose. Open your chest skywards and look up towards your left hand. To come out of the pose, inhale and lift your body up to standing and turn your feet parallel to each other. Repeat the pose on the other side.

Reverse Triangle Pose

Parivrtta Trikonasana ◆◆ medium pose

This posture creates a strong twist in the torso and back, helping to trim the waist, tone the abdomen, invigorate the abdominal organs and strengthen the back muscles. The rib cage is also turned, stimulating the lungs and improving respiration. You will feel your legs acting strongly to support all this work!

1 **Starting position** From Mountain Pose step your feet about 1.2m (4ft) apart, with feet parallel. Stretch your arms out to the sides at shoulder level.

2 **Lengthen your spine** and turn your left foot and leg in by 45°. Rotate your right leg and foot to the right by 90°, and turn your hips and torso to face to the right.

GENTLER VARIATION

Place your hand on the front of your ankle or shin, if reaching for the floor causes your knee to bend or your back to round.

3 **As you exhale,** draw your left arm and side of your body forwards and down to your right leg and right foot. Stretch your right arm up in line with your right shoulder and place your left hand on the floor by your right little toe (see Gentler Variation).

PRACTICE TIPS

When in the pose, strongly turn your hips, waist and chest to the right, whilst drawing your right hip back (and then your left hip when you repeat the pose). Lengthen your spine forwards and press your back outer heel deeply into the floor.

4 **Soften your shoulders** and draw them away from your ears. Take 5-10 breaths, opening your chest and looking up at your right hand. To come out of the pose, inhale and come back to standing and then turn your feet parallel to each other. Repeat the pose on the other side.

Warrior 1 Pose

Virabhadrasana 1   ◆◆ medium pose

Virabhadra is a mythical Indian warrior and the Warrior Poses are dedicated to him. They strengthen and harness energy within the body. Warrior 1 powerfully creates a sense of earthing as the feet, legs and hips become firmly rooted, whilst the waist, spine and chest lift up freeing the body of weight and tiredness.

1 **Starting position** From Mountain Pose step your feet about 1.2-1.4m (4-4½ft) apart and your feet parallel. Place your hands on your hips.

2 **Turn your left foot** and leg in by 45° and rotate your right leg and foot to the right by 90°. Turn your body to face to the right. Use your hands to gently draw your hip bones to face in the same direction.

GENTLER VARIATION

If your back knee feels strained or twisted in Step 4, release the back heel off the floor and brace your knee by drawing up the kneecap and surrounding muscles. If your shoulders start to hunch up, part your hands slightly and release your shoulders down.

4 **Lift your arms up** bringing the palms together over your head and bend your right leg fully so that your knee is now directly over your ankle, the shin is vertical and the thigh parallel to the floor. Look up at your hands and take 5-10 breaths. Let your tailbone sink and extend the back leg so the heel and foot are firmly on the floor. Inhale out of the pose. Repeat on the other side.

3 **Bend your right knee,** moving your leg into a right angle. Draw up both sides of your waist and lift your lower abdomen.

Warrior 2 Pose

Virabhadrasana 2 ◆◆ medium pose

In Warrior 2 Pose the hips are drawn open and the leg muscles stretched and worked deeply. As you maintain openness through the arms, the chest can greatly expand, allowing deeper breathing and improved blood circulation around the heart.

GENTLER VARIATION

At first your thigh muscles will feel the challenge of maintaining a right angle; do not strain to hold the pose. As your legs become stronger you will be able to hold the posture for longer.

1 **Starting position** From Mountain Pose step your feet about 1.2m-1.4m (4ft-4½) apart with your feet parallel. Turn the right leg and foot out to the right by 90° and the left leg and foot in by 15°; keep your body and head facing forwards. Inhale and extend your spine upwards with your arms stretching out to your fingertips at shoulder level.

2 **Slowly exhale and bend your right knee** over the right ankle, so your shin is vertical and your thigh is parallel to the floor as in Warrior 1. Press your left foot, especially the little toe edge, into the ground and lift your thigh muscles up. Look over your right hand and keep your shoulders relaxed. Take 5-10 breaths. Inhale and straighten your leg to come out of the pose and turn your feet parallel to each other. Repeat the pose on the other side.

PRACTICE TIPS

Don't allow your body to lunge over your bent leg or your hips to swing backwards. Draw your waist and spine up vertically and keep your bent knee pressing over towards your little toe. Feel your collarbones opening out to your fingertips.

Standing Forward Bend Pose

Uttanasana ◆ soft pose

The Standing Forward Bend Pose develops suppleness in the legs, hips and spine, whilst increasing the blood flow to the brain. For this reason it is a wonderfully refreshing posture and can be done at any time of day to relieve stiffness in the back, neck and shoulders. Take time to relax in this pose and you will find that your body yields deeper into the bend without forcing.

1 **Starting position** From Mountain Pose step your feet slightly apart, directly in line with your hips. Take care not to drop your arches. Lift your arms over your head and take each hand on to the opposite elbow. Inhale and draw up your knees, thighs, lower abdomen and spine.

PRACTICE TIPS

It is important to remember that forward bends move from the hips and not the waist. So towards the end of each out breath feel yourself relaxing and deepening the fold at the hips, keeping your legs strong.

2 **As you exhale,** extend your body forwards, hinging at the hips. Fold forwards and drop your head low. Take 10-20 breaths, relaxing and releasing tension from the back, shoulders and neck each time you breathe out.

3 **If your back** feels strained, bend your knees and rest the front of your ribs on your thighs.

GENTLER VARIATION

Stand in front of a wall or place a chair in front of you. In Step 1 place your hands on your hips then bend at the hips until your back is parallel with the floor. Bring your hands forwards to rest on the wall or chair at hip level and stretch the back forwards. If you suffer back pain, check with your doctor that this will be beneficial.

Downward Facing Dog Pose

Adho Mukha Svanasana ◆ soft pose

Downward Facing Dog Pose develops and balances upper and lower body strength. As the weight is taken off the back by the arms and legs, compression of the inter-vertebral discs is released and the entire spine is rejuvenated. Bringing the head low increases the blood flow to the brain and relieves mental fatigue. This is also a wonderful pose for runners and sportsmen and women as it stretches out the calf muscles which are prone to cramp.

1 Starting position
Come down on to your hands and knees with your knees directly under your hips and your hands in line with your shoulders, fingers pointing forwards. Spread your fingers and softly press your palms flat. Tuck your toes under and inhale feeling your spine long.

PRACTICE TIPS

In the full pose, breathe smoothly and lift your thighs, lower abdomen and hips up, whilst broadening your shoulders and sinking your heels. Pay attention to your hands and feet: press the palms of your hands down, stretching the middle fingers forwards. The soles of your feet extend into the floor while you continue to lift your arches.

GENTLER VARIATION

If your back feels strained in this pose, bend your knees slightly and move your body closer to your legs. Be aware that your heels will lift off the floor a fraction as you do this, but keep the pressure bearing down.

2 Exhale and strongly lift your hips up and backwards straightening your legs. Make sure your feet are parallel and press your heels down firmly. Bring your chin towards your chest and move the front of your torso towards your legs. Open into the pose for at least 10 breaths, then exhale and relax as you lower back down on to your knees.

Side Angle Pose

Parsvakonasana ◆◆/◆◆◆ medium/strong pose

Side Angle Pose develops length and tone throughout the sides of the body and builds stamina and endurance. It aids digestion, cleanses the system and relieves constipation. The pose also strengthens the legs as they control and maintain this strong lunge.

1 **Starting position** From Mountain Pose step your feet 1.2m (4ft) apart, with feet parallel. Turn your right leg and foot out to the right by 90° and the left foot and leg in by 15°. Stretch the arms out to the sides at shoulder level.

2 **Extend the soles of your feet** down into the floor, exhale and bend your right knee over your ankle to make a right angle. Lengthen your body to the side and place your right hand on the floor beside the little toe of your right foot. Lift your left arm up over your shoulder and take a breath or two here.

PRACTICE TIPS

During this pose do not lean your body forwards. Draw the upper side of your body back, turning your chest and face upwards. Press your right knee back against the right arm and open the soles of your feet down into the floor.

GENTLER VARIATION

If you are straining to reach the floor with your right hand, rest your elbow on top of your right thigh instead. Lift your left arm up over your shoulder, but don't drop your head.

3 **On your next exhalation turn the left arm** in its socket so the palm faces to the right and stretch it over by the side of your head. Soften your shoulder-blades down your back and look towards your left hand. Take 5-10 breaths. Inhale and lift your body out of the pose, turning your feet parallel to each other. Repeat the pose on the other side.

Side Extension Pose

Parsvottanasana ◆◆◆ strong pose

Side Extension Pose gives a fantastic stretch to the entire body, even the wrists and fingers are strongly involved! The backs of the thighs and the hips develop flexibility and any shoulder stiffness is soon released.

1 **Starting position** From Mountain Pose step your feet about 1.2-1.4m (4-4½ft) apart and stand firmly with your feet parallel. Take your hands behind your back and, bending your elbows, bring your palms together in a prayer position. Press your little fingers into your back and move your hands up between your shoulder-blades.

GENTLER VARIATION

If you can't bring the palms together, catch hold of your elbows instead.

2 **Turn your left foot and leg** in by 45° rotating your right leg and foot out to the right by 90°. Bring your hips and torso to face to the right. Inhaling, lengthen your spine and open your chest up.

3 **Slowly exhale** and stretch your back out and over your right leg, bringing your face towards your shin. Press your back foot into the ground whilst drawing the hip forwards. Gently squeeze the inner thighs towards one another and stay in the pose for 5-10 breaths. Inhale and lift your body up, releasing the pose and turning your feet parallel to each other. Repeat on the other side.

Tree Pose

Vrksasana ◆ soft pose

As you learn to hold the body in Tree Pose, the mind will become calmer and steadier. The balance is not just about standing on one leg, but is also the balance between the upwards stretch of the waist and arms and the firm downwards rooting of the leg and foot.

1 **Starting position** Stand in Mountain Pose then move your weight completely on to your left leg. Lift your right knee and gently hug it to your body.

2 **Rotating your right knee** out to the side, take hold of your right ankle and place the sole of your right foot against your upper, inner left thigh. Gently squeeze the foot and thigh together to secure the position.

GENTLER VARIATION

Balance comes with practice, and becoming tense as you try to achieve this pose will disturb the balance even more. Instead, just lower the foot and let your toes lightly hover above the floor. Lengthen your spine up, bend your elbows and press your palms softly together in prayer position.

3 **Bring your arms up** over your head, gently pressing your palms together and releasing your shoulders down. Breathe here for 10 breaths. Exhale and lower your arms and leg, then repeat the pose on the other side.

PRACTICE TIPS

As you hold the pose draw both sides of your waist up and lift your lower abdomen. Feel the sole of your standing foot softly opening into the floor and drop your tail-bone down.

Leg Stretch Pose

Prasarita Padottanasana ◆◆/◆◆◆ medium/strong pose

In Leg Stretch Pose your spine is elongated whilst the feet, ankles and legs work strongly to support this dynamic forward bend. This pose helps to strengthen the arches of the feet and align and define the muscles of the legs. It is also a good alternative to the headstand for those who are not yet comfortable with the head balance.

* In Step 3, don't attempt to walk your hands back through your legs if you feel any strain at all. For a gentler version, either remain in Step 2 of the pose, or practise Standing Forward Bend Pose on page 30.

1 **Starting position**
From Mountain Pose step your feet about 1.2-1.4m (4-4½ft) apart, with the feet parallel to each other.
Put your hands lightly on your hips. Inhale and lift your thigh muscles, waist, lower abdomen and spine.

2 **With an exhalation** extend your back forwards, folding at your hips and place your hands on the floor, fingers pointing forwards. Inhale and feel your back stretching out long and flat, with your chest broadening.

PRACTICE TIPS

Remember to keep your arches lifted in the full pose by pressing the outer edges of your feet down into the floor and drawing your knees and thighs up. Lift your buttock (sit) bones to deepen the pose. Keep your elbows in and no wider apart than your shoulders.

STRONGER VARIATION

As you get more familiar with this posture try interlacing your fingers and drawing your arms out, behind your back and head, to develop shoulder mobility and release tension.

3 **On an exhalation**
bend your elbows and walk your hands back through your legs. Fold your torso down and draw your head to the floor, whilst your shoulders lift away from the floor. Take 5-10 breaths, then inhale and slowly lift your body out of the pose.

Crescent Moon Pose

Anjaneyasana ◆◆◆ strong pose

Crescent Moon Pose is a beautiful posture which brings calmness and grace to the body and mind. It creates suppleness in the spine, openness in the pelvis and length in the legs. As the chest is drawn upwards the heart is stimulated, improving circulation and refreshing the entire body.

PRACTICE TIPS

As you hold the pose, open the toes of your back foot and press them into the floor to keep the leg and foot active. Drop your tailbone, and bring your weight forwards over the front leg, to stretch the back thigh and open the hips.

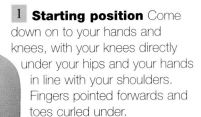

1 **Starting position** Come down on to your hands and knees, with your knees directly under your hips and your hands in line with your shoulders. Fingers pointed forwards and toes curled under.

2 **Step your right foot** in between your hands, drawing the hips forwards and bringing the weight over the right leg. Feel your left leg lengthen, but keep your knee on the floor. Keep your neck in line with your spine.

GENTLER VARIATION

You can place a cushion under your back knee if it feels uncomfortable against the floor. If arching your back creates tension in the spine, stretch up vertically instead.

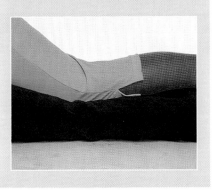

3 **Inhale and lift your body,** stretching your arms up and bringing the palms together. Lift the lower abdomen and chest as you gently arch back. Look towards your hands. Take 5-10 breaths in the pose, then inhale and lower your arms and return your hands to the floor. Step your right leg back, coming back to a hands and knees pose. Repeat the pose, bringing the left leg forwards.

Eagle Pose

Garudasana ◆◆ medium pose

With the legs and arms entwined in Eagle Pose, balance can be tricky. However, if we fully focus in this pose we can achieve a clear mind. As well as sharpening the mind the Eagle Pose opens up the back of the shoulders – which is a hot spot for stored tension.

1 **Starting position** Stand in Mountain Pose and wrap your arms over your chest with your fingers stretching over your shoulder-blades. Place the left arm over the right.

2 **Lift your hands up,** away from the shoulders, keeping the elbows snugly crossed. Bring your palms as close together as possible, lengthening your fingertips up whilst pressing the shoulders down. Take a couple of breaths.

GENTLER VARIATION

If your toes don't reach behind your calf to begin with, practise by pressing the little toe of the lifted foot against the ankle of the supporting leg.

PRACTICE TIPS

When you are in the pose, let your knees bend softly and deeply and remember to lengthen your spine. Keep gently releasing your shoulders back and down whilst your elbows slightly lift. Press your hands away from your face and feel your shoulder-blades opening.

3 **Exhale and bend both knees.** Balancing on your left foot, lift your right leg and cross it over the front of the left. Snake the right toes behind the left calf. Lift your lower abdomen and sink your tailbone, balancing and breathing in the pose for 5-10 breaths. As you inhale, release the legs and arms and come back to Mountain Pose. Repeat on the other side.

Happy Pose

Sukhasana ◆ soft pose

These two postures lay the foundations for all the other seated poses as they teach us to sit correctly with our body lengthened and centred over the pelvis. The principles of Happy and Staff Pose carry through all the other seated postures: that we need to sit evenly over the buttocks with the abdomen and lower back lifted, shoulders released down and the chest open, breathing steadily with a quiet mind.

1 **Starting position** Sit evenly on your buttocks, and cross your legs with your right shin over the left. Open your chest and keep your shoulders relaxed. Softly press your fingertips into the floor beside your hips and breathe length into your spine. Take 10-20 breaths.

PRACTICE TIPS

As you sit in Happy or Staff Pose, draw your lower back and abdomen up. Slide your shoulder-blades down to open your chest, and allow your collarbones to widen. Quieten the mind and listen to the evenness of your breath.

Staff Pose

Dandasana ◆ soft pose

1 **Starting position** Sit with your legs stretched out in front of you. Keep your legs straight and firm. Gently press your inner thighs and the inner edges of your feet together, whilst extending the soles of your feet away. Rest your hands beside your hips, with the fingers pointing forwards.

GENTLER VARIATION

If your back is weak it will hunch and round as you sit in Happy or Staff Pose. Try sitting on a block or firm cushion, or with your back against a wall to give you the extra support you need to maintain the poses.

Sitting Forward Bend Pose

Paschimottanasana ◆◆ medium pose

In this forward bend, the entire back of the body is gently stretched and drawn open from toe to head. This has a wonderful rejuvenating effect on the spine, and as the head and face are lowered, the focus is brought inwards, quietening, calming and relaxing the mind. Be careful not to force your body, instead focus on softening and surrendering into the forward bend.

1 Starting position From Staff Pose stretch your arms forwards, then exhale and lean your body forwards from the hips and catch hold of your toes. Don't hunch your shoulders or round your back. Breathe here, lengthening your spine and the back of your neck whilst drawing your chest up.

PRACTICE TIPS

Patience and a calm approach will help you with this pose. Do not struggle or force your body in any way. Keep your shoulders soft and your legs active. Lengthen the backs of your legs and press them down into the floor while gently drawing in your abdomen.

GENTLER VARIATION

If you lack flexibility, loop a strap or hand towel around the soles of your feet and sit on a block to enable the back to lengthen forwards. In Step 2, you can also place a cushion on your shins to rest your forehead on. This allows the body to become passive and relaxed and will help alleviate tension and headaches.

2 Exhale and fold deeply at the hips. Softly extend the front of your body out and over your legs and take your hands around the feet, bringing your forehead toward your shins. Take 10-20 breaths and then with a long, slow inhalation unfold back into Staff Pose.

Knee Head Pose

Janu Sirsasana ◆ soft pose

As you practise this pose, you will feel a tremendous stretch around the side and back of your waist. This activates the kidneys, thus aiding digestion, relieving constipation and cleansing the whole system. Extending the body over one leg at a time will help you identify if one leg is more tense or flexible than the other – and give you the chance to restore the balance.

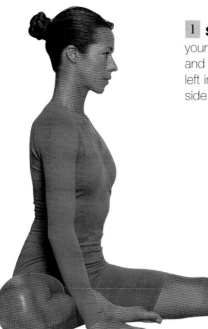

1 **Starting position** From Staff Pose bend your right knee and draw it back as far as possible and place the sole of your right foot against the left inner thigh. Allow the knee to fall out to the side. Inhale here and lengthen your spine.

PRACTICE TIPS

As you breathe in the pose, gently press the bent knee down to the floor and extend the other leg by pushing the heel away. Roll the side of the rib cage above the bent leg towards the inner thigh of the extended leg.

2 **Exhale and reach your hands forwards** to the left foot. Breathe here, lengthening your back and drawing your shoulders down.

GENTLER VARIATION

If you find it difficult to reach your foot with your hands, work with a strap or towel looped around the sole of your foot and sit on a firm cushion or block. (See Sitting Forward Bend, Gentler Variation, page 39.)

3 **On an out breath,** deepen the fold at your hips and draw your body forwards and over the left leg, the head extending beyond the knee. After 5-10 breaths inhale and lift the body up and come back to Staff Pose. Repeat the pose bending the left leg.

Knee Hug Pose

Supta Padangusthasana ◆◆ medium pose

With regular practice of the Knee Hug Pose your legs will gain in length, strength and flexibility. Lying on the floor provides your back with support, allowing the legs to be strongly but safely stretched without causing any strain to the back. This is an excellent posture for those who suffer from lower back tension and pain, as long as your doctor says that this would be beneficial.

1 **Starting position** Lie on your back with your legs stretched out and your inner thighs and the inner edges of your feet together.

PRACTICE TIPS

As you hold your toes keep the other leg and your back flat on the floor. Gently press the navel and shoulders down.

2 **As you exhale** bend your right knee up towards your chest. Hold your knee and gently draw your thigh into your body. Release your back and shoulders down into the floor and take 5-10 breaths.

3 **Using the index and middle fingers** of your right hand catch hold of your right big toe and with an exhalation, slowly straighten your leg keeping the back of the pelvis open on the floor. Take another 5-10 breaths, then bend your knee and hug it into your body again before relaxing it down to the floor. Repeat the pose bending and lifting your left leg.

GENTLER VARIATION

If you find it difficult to extend the leg while holding your toes, use a strap or towel looped around the foot instead. If you suffer from lower back pain you can also practise this pose by bending your left leg and placing the foot on the floor as you gently hug the right knee into your body. Extend the right leg right up if you feel comfortable doing so.

Half Lotus Stretch Pose

Ardha Padma Paschimottanasna ◆◆ medium pose

This is a deep pose and introduces the first stage of the Lotus Pose. By bending the knee and bringing the foot up to the opposite thigh you encourage suppleness in the knee and hip. Then as you lean the body forwards the heel gently presses into the lower abdomen, stimulating and toning the abdominal organs.

1 Starting position From Staff Pose, bend your right knee and bring your foot across to the very top of your left upper thigh, as if you were inserting your foot into the left hip socket. Draw the right knee in slightly towards the left. This is the first stage in developing the suppleness needed for the Lotus Pose.

2 Rest your fingertips on the floor beside your hips and take a few breaths, maintaining length in your back and keeping your chest open. Inhale and lift your arms then, as you exhale, lean your body forwards from your hips and catch hold of your left foot.

PRACTICE TIPS

Release this pose immediately if you experience any pain in your knees. Practise Knee Head Pose instead, until the knees become more supple and the hips more open.

3 On your next out breath softly deepen the fold at your hips and lengthen your body over your left leg. Bring your forehead towards your shin and take 5-10 breaths. Release the pose if you experience any pain in the knee, otherwise draw in your lower abdomen and relax the shoulders down from your ears. Extend the crown of your head toward the left ankle. As you inhale, lift the body up and come back to Staff Pose. Repeat the pose on the other side.

Lotus Pose

Padmasana ◆◆◆ strong pose

The Lotus Pose is a profound posture and can take years to master, thus teaching us patience and acceptance. For this reason a calm, gentle approach must be adopted when practising this pose. Lotus Pose develops mobility of the hips; be sure to bear this in mind so you do not try to force the pose by straining and over-stretching your knees.

1 Starting position
Sit in Happy Pose, then lift your right ankle and foot with both hands and gently bring the foot across to the very top of your left thigh.

2 This is Half Lotus Pose. Take a few breaths here and only continue if you feel ready and comfortable to do so.

3 Draw your left foot forward, and then with both hands take hold of the foot and ankle.

4 Bring your left foot and ankle up and over on to the very top of your right thigh. Draw your feet in closer to the hips and softly rest your hands on your knees. Lengthen your spine and take 5-10 breaths. With an exhalation release the legs and return to Happy Pose. Repeat bringing the left foot in first.

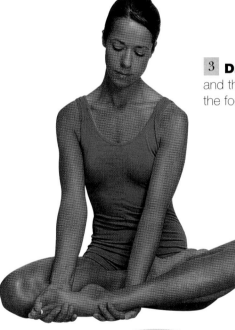

PRACTICE TIPS

If you suffer from knee problems or experience any pain in the knee at all, stop immediately and assume Happy Pose instead. Practising Half Lotus, where only one foot is placed over the thigh, will also be beneficial for those with tightness in the hips and knees. Be sure to practise Half Lotus on both sides to create balance.

43

Cow Face Pose

Gomukhasana ◆◆ medium pose

Cow Face Pose creates a fantastic opening and release around the shoulders and upper arms and is particularly beneficial to those who suffer from tense and rounded shoulders. The elbow lifts sharply, resembling the sharpness of a cow's horns.

1 **Starting position** Bend your knees and sit on your heels, keep your spine lifted. Bend your left arm at the elbow, reaching the back of your hand and fingers up your back towards your right shoulder blade. Stretch your right arm up without lifting your shoulders.

GENTLER VARIATION

If you find it hard to clasp your hands, use a strap held in the hand reaching down to link your hands. If sitting on your heels is uncomfortable, place a cushion between your thighs and calves.

PRACTICE TIPS

Draw your lifted elbow backwards by the side of the head, and move both shoulder-blades in and down. Open the chest and lift the lower abdomen while relaxing the face.

2 **Bend the right elbow** and reach your fingers down to catch hold of your left fingers. Take 5-10 breaths extending your left elbow down and your right elbow up. Slowly release the clasp of the hands and repeat the pose reaching your right arm behind your back.

Cobbler Pose

Baddha Konasana ◆ soft pose

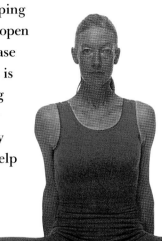

Both Cobbler and Sleeping Cobbler Pose help to open up the hip joints and release tension from the pelvis. It is an exceptionally comforting posture to practise during menstruation or pregnancy and is recommended to help strengthen the bladder.

1 Starting position Sit on a firm cushion or block to give extra lift to your back and bring the soles of your feet together, bending your knees out and down to the sides. Place your heels as close as possible to your pubic bone and softly press your fingertips into the floor slightly behind your hips, with the fingers facing towards your body. Breathe steadily allowing your knees to drop towards the floor.

2 Place your hands gently on your ankles, keeping your back long and straight over your pelvis. Draw your collarbones wide and your shoulders down. Take 5-10 breaths in the pose, then release the legs out of the pose.

Sleeping Cobbler Pose

Supta Baddha Konasana ◆ soft pose

1 From Cobbler Pose place your finger-tips on the floor behind your hips and, keeping the soles of your feet together, lower your back to the floor or on to a cushion. Bring your arms over your head and loosely clasp your hands. Relax and take up to 30 breaths. To come out of the pose draw your knees across to the right, roll to the right and gently come off the cushion.

PRACTICE TIPS

In both Cobbler and Sleeping Cobbler Pose relax the inner thighs and underside of the legs to gently open out the hips. The abdomen remains softly lifted.

GENTLER VARIATION

If your back and hips are stiff you can practise Cobbler Pose with your back against a wall and a cushion in between the wall and the back of your waist. As your back gains strength, you will be able to dispense with these supports.

Seated Angle Pose

Upavista Konasana ◆◆◆ strong pose

This pose has revitalizing benefits for the entire body. It helps free up energy within the pelvis and improves circulation down into the legs and feet, whilst strengthening the back muscles. It creates length in the legs and flexibility in the hips. Seated Angle Pose is also a balancing posture that is good to practise during menstruation as it regulates the flow.

1 **Starting position** From Staff Pose take your legs out to the sides, taking your feet as wide apart as you can. Stretch your legs, pressing the heels away and making sure your toes and knees face upwards. With your waist, abdomen and spine drawn up, place your fingertips on the floor behind your hips and relax your shoulders. Take a few breaths.

PRACTICE TIPS

Whilst holding the pose, maintain a lift in your lower abdomen to support the lower back. Keep the legs active by drawing the thigh muscles towards the hips and stretching the heels away. Move the pubic bone down and back to increase the forward bend.

2 **Exhale and lean** your body forwards, moving from your hips and lengthening your back. Reach your hands down to your shins, press the chest open and the shoulders back. Breathe calmly.

3 If you are able to do so comfortably, lengthen your body further forwards, taking hold of your big toes. Lean your chest to the floor and broaden your shoulders out. Take 5-10 breaths then, when you feel ready, inhale and lift your body out of the pose.

GENTLER VARIATION

Work gently in this pose so as not to strain the inner thighs or groin. Sitting on a firm cushion or block will help you extend your lower back. If you can't reach your toes keep the palms on the shins or ankles instead.

Another gentle way to practise this posture is to do the Inverted Practice Forms, Step 2 (page 58) instead.

Little Boat Twist

Supta Parivartanasana ◆ soft pose

This is a wonderfully soothing twist. The whole body is supported on the floor which makes it particularly helpful for releasing tightness and tension throughout the back and shoulders without risk of strain. The longer you breathe and rest into this twist on each side, softening into the floor, the deeper the benefits of Little Boat Twist.

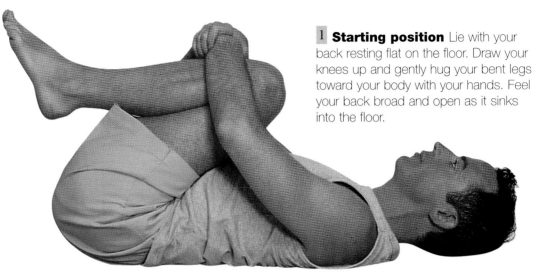

1 Starting position Lie with your back resting flat on the floor. Draw your knees up and gently hug your bent legs toward your body with your hands. Feel your back broad and open as it sinks into the floor.

PRACTICE TIPS

As you relax in the pose (steps 3 and 4) let your body soften, opening the back of your shoulders and arms down to the floor. Relax the top leg heavily on the leg underneath.

2 Stretch your arms out to the sides at shoulder level, palms facing up. Keep your shoulders relaxed and the back of your neck long.

3 **As you exhale, draw your knees across to the right side,** keeping your knees together. Relax your legs allowing them to rest heavily on the floor. Turn your head and look towards your left hand. Relax in the pose for 5-10 breaths.

4 **Exhale, roll on to your back** and bring your knees up. Take a breath or two then, on your next exhalation, take your knees across to the left side. Turn your head to look towards your right hand. Relax in the pose for 5-10 breaths. To come out of the pose, exhale and softly roll on to your back.

GENTLER VARIATION

If this twist feels too strong, place a cushion on the floor to rest your knees on. You can also lie with a cushion under your head if your neck is particularly stiff or tender.

Half Twisting Fish

Ardha Matsyendrasana ◆◆◆ strong pose

This intricate twist trims the waistline, develops full spinal rotation and relieves tension in the lower, middle and upper back. It creates length in the neck and freedom in the shoulders, whilst improving digestion.

* As in all twists be sure to lengthen your spine first and then twist, so as not to compress or grind your vertebrae.

1 **Starting position** From Staff Pose bend your right knee and bring your foot across to the very top of your left upper thigh. (See Half Lotus Stretch Pose page 42.) Rest your fingertips lightly on the floor beside your hips and extend your spine upwards.

3 **Exhale and draw your left shoulder back** and extend your left fingertips towards your right shin and reach your right hand forwards and take hold of your left big toe. Take 5-10 breaths then inhale and come back to Staff Pose. Repeat the posture on the other side.

2 **Exhale and turn to the left** placing your right hand on the outside of your left leg and reach your left fingertips towards your right, inner thigh. Breathe for a few moments, opening your chest.

GENTLER VARIATION

If you feel any strain in your bent knee, place your foot on the floor by your left inner thigh, instead of on top of your thigh. Practise twisting from this position without taking your right hand to the left foot and leaving the fingertips of your left hand on the floor by your right hip.

PRACTICE TIPS

To develop this pose keep taking your left shoulder back and draw both shoulder-blades down. To begin with, your fingers may not reach your shin so work with the hand at the inner thigh. With practice, suppleness will come and the fingers will slip down to the shin.

Sage's Twist

Marichyasana ◆◆ medium pose

This pose is named after Marichya, the ancient Indian sage and grandfather of the sun god. Through the practice of this twist, tension is released from the lower back, and the chest and shoulders are opened. The internal organs are massaged and stimulated, in particular the liver, spleen and intestines.

* Always be sure to lengthen your spine first and then twist, so as not to compress or grind your vertebrae.

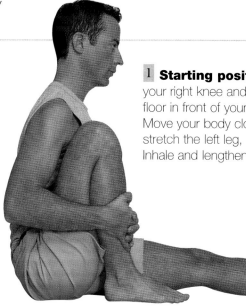

1 **Starting position** From Staff Pose, bend your right knee and place your right foot on the floor in front of your right buttock (sit) bone. Move your body close to the bent leg and stretch the left leg, pushing the heel away. Inhale and lengthen your spine.

PRACTICE TIPS

Do not lean the back backwards, keep the spine lifting up on a vertical line and release the shoulder-blades down.

2 **Exhale and turn the front of your body toward the right leg.** Wrap your left arm around your bent knee and take your right hand back on to the floor behind your hips. As you take 5-10 breaths here, draw your right collarbone and shoulder back bringing your chin over your right shoulder. Inhale and release from the twist coming back to Staff Pose. Repeat the posture on the other side.

GENTLER VARIATION

Another way to practise Sage's Twist is to sit sideways on a chair. Lengthen your spine, exhale and rotate your body bringing your hands to rest on the back support of the chair.

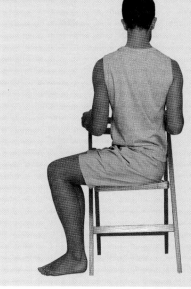

Locust Pose

Salabhasana ◆ soft pose

The Locust Pose powerfully develops strength throughout the entire back and so is an ideal remedy for spinal weakness. It creates tone in the back of the legs and pelvis, so it is a good pose for beginners to start back-bending postures with.

1 **Starting position** Lie on your front with your chin on the floor and stretch your body long from head to toe. Place your arms by your sides with the palms of your hands facing up.

PRACTICE TIPS

As you hold the pose, draw your shoulders back and shoulder-blades in, feeling the heart lifting. Keep the legs strong and straight whilst pressing inner thighs, inner knees, inner ankles and big toes together.

2 **Inhale and lift your head**, shoulders, chest and legs up off the floor. Stretch the toes and fingers back and press the backs of your hands down on to the floor. Take 5-10 breaths and then with an exhalation relax the body down.

GENTLER VARIATION

If lifting both the upper body and legs at the same time causes strain in your back, practise the pose by lifting the upper body first. Release the body down then practise lifting the legs. As your back gains strength, lifting the upper body and legs together into this pose will soon become achievable.

Cobra Pose

Bhujangasana ◆◆ medium pose

Regular practice of Cobra Pose awakens the flow of energy through the spine and tones the nerves, creating clearer communication between body and mind. It helps to realign the spine and encourages correct vertebral placement.

1 **Starting position** Lie on the front of your body, with the palms of your hands open on the floor underneath your shoulders and your elbows drawn in. Stretch your legs out behind you.

PRACTICE TIPS

Do not strain in Cobra Pose. Focus on arching evenly through your spine, drawing your shoulders back and down whilst lifting your chest up. Draw your tailbone in and feel the back of your pelvis open.

2 **Inhale and press down on your hands,** lengthening your spine forwards and up. Work towards straightening the arms without hunching up your shoulders. Lift your head and open your chest and breathe steadily for 5-10 breaths. On an exhalation bend the elbows and relax your body to the floor.

GENTLER VARIATION

Back bends must be taken slowly, steadily building up strength and flexibility, so if you suffer pain or tightness in the lower back in this pose, do not straighten your arms. Keep your forearms on the floor and practise this position until the back feels supple enough to progress to the full pose.

53

Bridge Building Pose

Setu Bandhasana ◆ soft pose

The Bridge Building Pose develops the required strength in the legs to support the bending of the back in all back-bending postures. As the front of the body is drawn up, the abdominal organs are stimulated and the colon is opened aiding digestion.

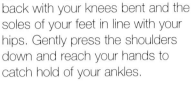
1 Starting position Lie on your back with your knees bent and the soles of your feet in line with your hips. Gently press the shoulders down and reach your hands to catch hold of your ankles.

2 Inhale and press your feet strongly into the floor, raising the pelvis and back up. Arch through your spine and lift your chest towards your chin. Take 5-10 even breaths, then exhale, release your ankles and bring the back down on to the floor.

PRACTICE TIPS

Work your legs dynamically in the pose by keeping your thighs, knees and feet parallel to each other. Draw your shoulder-blades in and press the shoulders down whilst softening the back of your neck into the floor.

GENTLER VARIATION

If you find it difficult to reach your ankles when you first practise Bridge Building Pose, simply interlace your fingers and stretch your arms away from your shoulders as you lift your pelvis and back from the floor.

Camel Pose

Ustrasana ◆◆◆ *strong pose*

The Camel Pose is a most exhilarating posture which opens and stretches the thigh muscles, hips, abdomen, ribs, chest and neck. It tones the legs and buttocks, whilst improving respiration as the lungs are expanded. Stiffness in the neck and shoulders is alleviated as the weight of the head is released back.

1 **Starting position** Kneel on the floor with your knees hip width apart and your hands on the back of your pelvis. Lengthen your spine.

PRACTICE TIPS

Keep the abdomen lifted and your thighs strong as you maintain the pose. Your hips need to move forwards directly over your knees. Press your shin bones down into the floor.

GENTLER VARIATION

If you experience any tension in your back while you do this pose use a chair, with a bolster for padding, on which to arch your back.

2 **Move your hips forwards,** lifting your chest and softly arching your back. Lift your lower abdomen as you move the tailbone in and down.

3 **Exhale and release your shoulders back,** opening your chest up and reaching your hands down on to the soles of your feet. Release the neck muscles allowing your head to drop back. Take 5-10 breaths, increasing the arch with each breath.

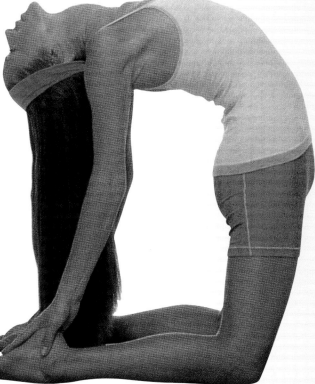

Plough Pose

Halasana ◆ soft pose

The Plough Pose is an ideal posture for awakening the spine and relieving tension in the neck, shoulders and back. It helps alleviate fatigue and headaches.

* Don't practise inverted poses if menstruating or suffering from high blood pressure, heart problems or neck injuries.

1 **Starting position** Lie with your back and shoulders on a folded blanket or yoga mat and with your head on the floor. Bend your knees, place your feet on the floor and extend your arms close to the sides of your body, pressing your shoulders and the palms of your hands down.

2 **Exhale and roll your hips up** and off the floor, bending your knees over your face. Move your elbows and shoulder-blades inwards, and place the palms of your hands on the back of your waist keeping your elbows on the floor. Take a few even breaths.

3 **Exhale, straighten your legs** and reach your toes down to the floor beyond your head. Bring your chest forwards to touch your chin. Interlace your fingers behind your back, gently pressing your little fingers down on the floor and straightening the arms. Breathe steadily for 10-30 breaths. Exhale and release the pose by softly rolling your back, like a ball, back down to the floor.

PRACTICE TIPS

As you breathe in the pose draw in your lower abdomen and move your hips up and over your shoulders. Feel your legs extending out of your hips as the tips of your toes touch the floor. Do not tense the shoulders, neck or face.

GENTLER VARIATION

If taking your feet to the floor causes strain or discomfort in the neck, shoulders, back or head, position a chair just behind your head and bring your legs down very carefully to rest on the seat.

Shoulderstand

Sarvangasana ◆◆ medium pose

The Shoulderstand is often referred to as the Mother Pose. It soothes and nourishes the entire body and strengthens the nervous system. With the legs raised, tired feet are revived and varicose veins prevented. It has a cleansing effect on digestion, as the thyroid gland (in the front of the throat) is stimulated and the metabolism balanced.

* Don't practise inverted poses if menstruating or suffering from high blood pressure, heart problems or neck injuries.

1 Starting position From Plough Pose, bend your elbows and place the palms of your hands firmly on the back of your ribs. Lift your toes off the floor, bending the knees and bringing your feet over the buttocks.

2 Extend your legs and stretch your feet and toes up so that the body is vertical. Feel the back of your head, shoulders and elbows releasing down into the ground. Lift the lower abdomen up and in and spread the soles of your feet open. Breathe steadily for 10-30 breaths – over time build up to staying here for 2-3 minutes. Exhale and bend your knees down, returning to Plough Pose. Take a few breaths then exhale and slowly roll the back down to the floor.

EAGLE VARIATION

There are many lovely variations to the Shoulderstand which you may want to try once you feel comfortable with Plough Pose and Shoulderstand. Practise taking the legs into Eagle Pose by wrapping the left leg over the right and then the right leg over the left.

PRACTICE TIPS

Work to maintain a vertical alignment of the body in Shoulderstand by lifting from the root of the pose, the neck and shoulders. Balance on the tops of your shoulders and move your chest up to your chin. Press your palms into the back of your ribs, floating your pelvis and tailbone up.

Inverted Practice Forms

Viparita Karani ◆ soft pose

This series of inverted postures relieves fatigue in the legs and feet, and allows the back to align with the floor. As the feet are lifted higher than the heart, circulation is improved whilst the body rests. During menstruation or if you suffer from high blood pressure, heart problems or neck injuries, it is advised not to practise inversions (Plough Pose, Shoulderstand, Headstand). These Inverted Practice Forms provide a superb alternative.

1 **Starting position** Lie on your right side with your buttocks against a wall. Roll on to your back and stretch your legs up the wall (see picture, right). Keep your legs together. Feel your back relaxing and releasing into the floor, whilst gently extending your heels up, away from your hips. Take 10-30 breaths.

PRACTICE TIPS

Let your body relax completely, gently sinking the back into the floor with each out breath. Keep the chin level so the back of the neck remains lengthened.

2 **Exhale and open your legs**, drawing your feet apart – keep the back of the knees open against the wall. Breathe evenly in this pose for 10-30 breaths.

GENTLER VARIATION

If you experience back pain, place a few folded blankets under your pelvis to support the lower back as you practise these poses.

3 **Relax your hips as you exhale,** bend your knees and draw the soles of your feet together. Take 10-30 breaths, then bring your knees together and roll on to your right side to come out of the pose.

Fish Pose

Matsyasana ◆ soft pose

This pose is the counter pose to the Shoulderstand and Plough Pose as it releases the neck and shoulders, and lengthens out the throat which is compressed during the other two postures. It also expands the chest and lifts the heart. Remember to always practise Fish Pose after the Shoulderstand.

1 **Starting position** Lying on your back, keep your feet on the floor and bend your knees. Inhale and lift your hips up. Bring your arms underneath your body. Draw your elbows and shoulder-blades in towards one another.

2 **Exhale and lower your body down on top of your arms**. Press the palms of your hands flat on the floor, keeping the thumbs together. Stretch your legs away and take a breath or two here.

PRACTICE TIPS

As you hold Fish Pose draw your collarbones wide and your spine up into your body to increase the arch of your back.

3 **Inhale and raise your chest up**, pressing down firmly on your elbows. Draw the crown of your head on to the floor. Keep your legs and feet together whilst extending your heels away. Take 5-10 breaths and feel the front of your body opening, then exhale and relax the back down to the floor, release the arms from underneath you and come out of the pose.

GENTLER VARIATION

If your back feels tense you can practise Fish Pose by lying over a bolster with your arms over your head, see Sleeping Cobbler Pose (page 45). Stretch your legs out and keep them together.

Headstand

Sirsasana ◆◆◆ strong pose

Ancient texts talk of the Headstand as the king and father of all postures. As the blood is drawn from the heart and flows through the brain it clears the mind creating clarity and mental vitality. It is an empowering pose developing strength and confidence on a physical, emotional and mental level.

* Don't practise inverted poses if menstruating or suffering from high blood pressure, heart problems or neck injuries.

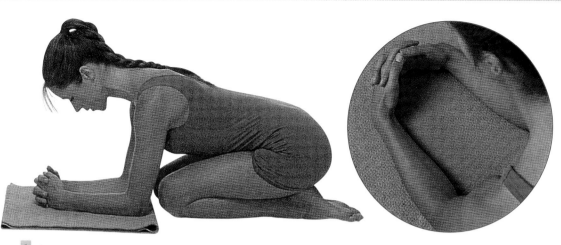

1 Starting position Kneel in front of a folded yoga mat with your knees together. Place your forearms on the mat, with your elbows in line with your shoulders just by the knees. Cup your hands and interlace your fingers, with your little fingers on the floor.

2 Exhale and lower the top of your head on to the mat, bringing the back of your head into the palms of your cupped hands. Tuck your toes under and strongly lift your shoulders up, away from your ears. Press your forearms and elbows firmly down into the mat as your supporting base.

3 Inhale, straighten your legs and walk your feet in toward your face. Lift your abdomen and raise your hips directly over your shoulders and head.

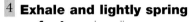

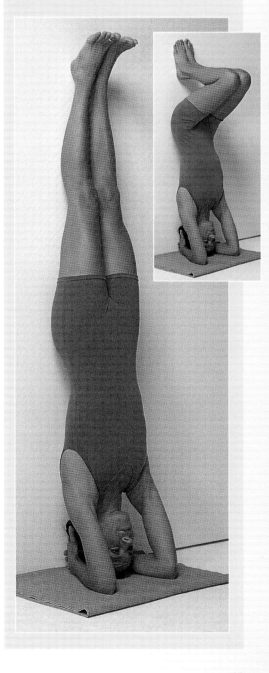

4 Exhale and lightly spring your feet up, bending your knees and taking your heels toward your buttocks. Balance evenly over your forearms, elbows and head whilst drawing your shoulders up, away from the floor. Breathe calmly in this position. Once you feel steady and strong at this stage – continue to the next position.

GENTLER VARIATION

When you first try the Headstand it may help you to practise against a wall. When you are in the pose start moving your hips and legs away from the wall, so that you gradually build up the strength and confidence to balance unaided.

PRACTICE TIPS

In the same way that placing the feet correctly creates the foundations for good standing postures, the Headstand relies on a solid base created by the position of your elbows under your shoulders. To balance properly keep your weight evenly distributed between your arms.

5 As you breathe evenly, slowly lengthen your legs opening the soles of your feet towards the ceiling. When you first practise this pose, hold it for 5-10 breaths, then as you gain confidence stay in the pose for 2-3 minutes or for as long as it feels comfortable. To come out of the Headstand, bend your knees in and down towards the chest. Then stretch the legs down extending the toes on to the floor. Bend the knees and rest your body in Child's Pose (see page 64) for 10-20 breaths.

spirit

Closing Your Practice

The following postures bring our physical practice to a close, evoking a sense of completion and calm and allowing the body and mind to become receptive to relaxation. Taking this time to wind down is essential in creating a balanced practice and an internal harmony.

In yoga philosophy it is believed that spiritual energy, or *kundalini*, which is often depicted as a coiled serpent, lies sleeping at the base of the spine. This dormant energy is awakened through the practice of yoga postures and breathing techniques, as the nerve channels of the spine are purified through the yoga movements and the cleansing effects of the breath. Towards the end of your practice you may notice a change in your mood and state of being – a restored sense of calm, ease, clarity and heightened perception – this is yoga at work, a subtle awakening of spiritual consciousness.

The final poses seal in this consciousness and provide an opportunity for reflection and introspection: encouraging a quietening of the mind so we can start to listen inwardly with this newly aroused spiritual and divine awareness and energy.

Relaxation and Surrender

Relaxation is essential for good health, vitality and peace of mind. When we truly relax, our whole being is replenished and a wealth of energy and creativity is released. Our mental state is intrinsically linked to our physical condition. When our minds are troubled or anxious so too are our bodies. When our minds are calm, balanced and happy this is reflected in our physical well-being. Tension and stress are part of life, and we all experience them in varying degrees. They not only accumulate in our minds but also in our muscles, joints and organs – including the heart. If we neglect the necessity of relaxing and releasing stress and tension they slowly build up and tighten our body, mind and heart.

Child's Pose

Mudhasana

This is a wonderfully soothing posture which gently extends and lengthens the spine, helping to bring the breath in to the back of the lungs and body. It is a perfect pose to rest in after the Headstand (page 60).

1 **Starting position** Kneel on the floor with your knees together and sit back on your heels. Bring your forehead to the ground and softly extend your arms back so your hands are resting by your feet with the palms facing up. Soften and relax your body and stay in the pose for as long as you feel comfortable.

GENTLER VARIATION

If you have restricted mobility in your hips or knees, try leaning your body over a bolster or large cushion.

Yoga Sealing Pose

Yoga Mudrasana

Mudras are symbolic gestures, which are either performed with the hands or the whole body in order to promote positive energy flow within the body. *Yoga Mudrasana* is often used to close the yoga practice before relaxation as it harnesses the benefits of the previous *asanas* and helps to awaken spiritual energy.

1 **Starting position** Sit in Happy Pose (page 38), Half Lotus Pose or Lotus Pose (page 43). Inhale, lengthen your spine and interlock your fingers behind your back.

2 **As you exhale softly lean your body forwards,** taking your head down towards the floor. Draw your arms up and take 5-10 breaths, concentrating on releasing the back of your neck, spine and shoulders.

3 **Inhale and bring your head and body upright again.** Place your hands on your knees feeling the length in your back. Relax your shoulders and breathe softly and evenly for 5-10 breaths.

GENTLER VARIATION

Soften the Yoga Sealing Pose by sitting in Happy Pose (page 38) and catching hold of your elbows behind your back, rather than interlacing your fingers.

Corpse Pose
Savasana

In *Savasana* you let troubles go and allow your body to relax deeply. Stay in Corpse Pose for up to 15 minutes as proper relaxation is more of a process than a position. It is a conscious letting go and a gradual releasing of tension layer by layer.

It's important to keep warm whilst in *Savasana*, so either spread a blanket over yourself or put on extra clothing that is not restrictive.

1 **Starting position** Lie on the ground with your arms a little way out from the sides of your body and your feet slightly wider apart than your hips. Allow yourself to become comfortable and close your eyes.

2 **Listen to your breath.** With each exhalation let your whole body sink heavily into the ground. With each inhalation feel the breath drawing deep into your lungs as your belly and navel softly rise.

3 **Breath by breath**, let your whole self relax.

4 **Rest here for 10 minutes.** When your mind wanders, gently bring your attention back to the steady soft flow of your breathing. When you are ready to come out of the pose roll slowly and gently on to your right side. Draw your knees in loosely and take a few breaths, then come to a sitting position using your hands to help you up.

PRACTICE TIPS

Try not to move in Savasana *as this will cause distraction rather than relaxation. Make sure you are comfortable to begin with.*

GENTLER VARIATIONS

If you have lower back ache or find lying flat uncomfortable, bend your knees and place your feet hip distance apart. If keeping the knees bent causes the leg muscles to remain partly active, place a bolster under your knees. You can also use a firm pillow or block under your head if you suffer from neck pain or stiffness.

Breathing
Pranayama

From the moment of birth to the moment of death breath flows through our bodies, nourishing each and every cell. It is our fuel for life and, for this reason, breath is the essence of yoga. Pranayama, *which literally means extending vital energy, provides breathing practices which refine our breath and the flow of life's energy within us.*

The ancient text, the Hatha yoga pradipika, *states that he who only half breathes only half lives, and so in order to live fully we need to breathe fully. This supports the traditional yogic belief that it is not the number of years lived which* determine the length of our lives, but the number of breaths taken. Today it is recognized that by slowing our breathing down we can reduce stress levels, which benefits the heart.

Notice, for example, how your breathing quickens when you are stressed, or you may even hold your breath. Shallow breathing causes a build up of old stagnant air in our lungs, limiting the amount of air we can take in and depriving the body of fresh oxygen. This way of breathing often becomes a habit, and so through yoga we learn to let these habits go and through **Pranayama** *we start to breathe fully again.*

Watching the Breath
Pranayama

Pranayama *practice can be done 20 minutes after* asana *practice or an hour before – or you may wish to do it on its own. Observe the same cautions and guidelines as* asana *practice. Start* Pranayama *by simply observing the breath.*

PRACTICE TIPS
When you first practise **Pranayama** *your mind will wander. Relax and gently return your focus to the sound and feel of each in and out breath.*

1 **Starting position** Lie on your back with your eyes closed and your hands softly resting on your belly. Feel the movement of your abdomen as you breathe through your nose, with your mouth closed.

2 **Start to notice the quality of your breathing.** Without changing it, become aware of where the breath is going to in your body. Is the breath coarse or smooth, short or long, shallow or deep, fast or slow – or somewhere in between?

3 **As you continue to breathe** see your breath as light. Let it flow in through your nose, down your throat, through your chest and into your lungs. From here it gently glows outwards, spreading throughout your body.

4 **As you exhale** see the journey of your breath in reverse as your lungs empty completely, creating space for the new breath.

5 **Stay here, deepening the awareness of your breath** and stay in this position for about 2 minutes. Gradually build up to 10-15 minutes practice.

FOCUSING ON YOUR BREATH

As you become more familiar with watching and listening to your breath, you will notice a subtle change, or slight retention, as you change from inhalation to exhalation and vice versa. This is the moment when one breath has completed and before the next breath has started. This natural retention is called *kumbhaka*. Do not hold this retention, simply notice it.

Practise mindful breathing whilst sitting in Happy Pose (page 38), Half Lotus Pose (page 43) or sitting on a chair.

Victorious Breath
Ujjayi Pranayama

As *Ujjayi Pranayama* is practised your breath becomes audible as it gently resonates through a slightly contracted throat. This has a calming effect on the nervous system and helps to keep the mind focused as it follows the soft even sound of the *ujjayi* breath.

1 **Starting position** Sit in Happy Pose (page 38), Half Lotus Pose (page 43) or on a chair and join your hands in prayer position (left) or place them on your knees (below). Relax your breath and remain here for a few moments breathing softly. As you continue to breathe, gently contract the back of your throat so that a soft 'haaa' sound can be heard as you inhale and exhale.

PRACTICE TIPS

When you feel comfortable with the Victorious Breath you can use ujjayi *breathing as you practise your postures, then you will be able to hear when you are straining or holding your breath.*

2 **Take 6-12 long** slow *ujjayi* breaths, then lie on the floor and relax. The breath must not feel strained. If it does, stop and rest.

SUCCESSFUL **UJJAYI** BREATHING

If you have difficulty creating the 'haaa' sound of the *ujjayi* breath, start by breathing in and out of your slightly open mouth whilst making the sound. When the 'haaa' sounds evenly on both the inhalation and exhalation, gently close your mouth and continue breathing with the 'haaa' sound as the breath now flows in and out of the nose. The sound will change slightly but the 'haaa' sound remains audible.

Meditation and Hand Gestures
Dhyana and Mudras

Meditation is an ancient practice that has wonderful restorative powers, and brings about inner balance, clarity and peace. Meditation, or dhyana, is an important aspect of our practice and is the seventh limb of yoga (pages 10-11). It is a process which opens our minds and our very selves to universal consciousness and leads us to samadhi, *the blissful state of enlightenment.*

Universal life flow, vital energy or prana *is most apparent in stillness, and so in meditation we bring ourselves to sit quietly in order to connect to this deep and full awareness.*

However, this is not always easy, as our minds tend to be constantly full of chatter, plans, worries, anxieties, memories, wishes, dreams, desires, and regrets. In meditation, we practise noticing these thoughts without getting caught up in the drama of them all. This can give us a fresh perspective as we begin to let go and relax with everything just as it is. Start with just five minutes meditation and build up gradually.

The Mudras, *symbolic gestures, shown here are one of the tools that help us with meditation. They give the mind a focal point and redirect energy released through the hands back into the body, creating circuits or loops of energy.*

When you start to meditate, thoughts will be bound to crowd in. Be kind and patient with yourself, notice and recognize these thoughts, then let them go; again, and again, and again.

Gesture of the Seven Gates
Shanmukhi Mudra

Pratyahara, which means withdrawal, is the fifth limb of yoga (pages 10-11) as outlined in the *Yoga Sutras,* and is a preparation for meditation. Withdrawing our focus, from the external world to the internal self, develops a sense of inner quiet and calm. *Shanmukhi Mudra* helps us to look and listen inwardly to the source of our being.

1 **Starting position** Sit in Happy Pose (page 38), or Lotus Pose (page 43) or on a chair, resting the backs of your hands on your knees. Take a few soft, even breaths.

2 **Lift your hands to your face** and lightly place your index fingers just below your eyebrows, your middle fingers on your eyelids, your ring fingers on your outer nostrils and your little fingers by your upper lip (right).

3 **Gently press your thumbs** against your ears, whilst very softly and slightly drawing your index fingers up toward your eyebrows and the middle fingers down toward the eyelashes.

4 **Keep the pressure of your fingers** sensitive and even. Breathe here for as long as feels comfortable and allow yourself to feel an inner stillness that comes as your senses retreat.

5 **To come out of *Shanmukhi Mudra*** slowly lower your hands and arms and remain in this calm state for another 10-20 breaths.

Focused Gazing
Trataka

Watching the breath, as you do in *Pranayama*, develops your concentration or *dharana* – the sixth limb of yoga (pages 10-11). *Trataka* is another technique in concentration. In *Pranayama* the mind is focused on the breath, whilst in *Trataka* it is focused on an object. A lit candle is a good starting point.

1 Starting position Sit in Happy Pose (page 38), Lotus Pose (page 43) or on a chair. Place a lit candle at eye level or a little below, about 1m (3ft) away, and take a few slow, even breaths.

2 Take your focus to the candle. Do not strain your eyes, keep your gaze steady and relaxed. Absorb the image and then, after a minute, close your eyes and continue to see the flame in your mind's eye.

3 When the image fades, open your eyes and focus again on the flame. Repeat the process for as long as feels comfortable.

Gesture of Knowledge
Chin Mudra

This is the most well-known hand gesture of yoga, and symbolizes the individual consciousness (index finger) touching and connecting to the universal consciousness (thumb). This represents the ultimate aim of yoga, which is complete union.

Starting position Sit in Happy Pose (page 38) or any other comfortable sitting position. Lengthen your back, and release your shoulders down. Relax your face.

Place your index fingers to the pads of your thumbs, turn the palms up and rest the backs of your hands on the tops of your knees.

Quieten your mind and follow your breath.

Feel your breath circling from your nose through your body to your hands, then back again as you breathe out.

Let yourself become absorbed in this circling energy and breathe calmly for as long as feels comfortable. Build up your duration to 15-30 minutes.

Gesture of the Heart
Hridaya Mudra

This hand position draws energy, or *prana*, that has travelled out to the hands, back in towards the heart. On a physical level, it strengthens and revitalizes the cardio muscle of the heart, and on an emotional level it is said to release and unburden the heart of sadness and sorrow.

Starting position Sit comfortably. Lift your spine and relax your shoulders and face.

Curl your index fingers under your thumbs, and place your middle and ring fingers to the tip of your thumbs. Extend your little fingers and rest the backs of your hands on your knees.

Breathe evenly, feeling your heart open and expand with each in breath. With each out breath feel the heart release unwanted emotion. Take time to experience the sensation of each breath.

To close your meditation, bring your palms together in prayer position, take a few breaths then release hands and legs.

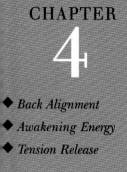
living yoga

Yoga Sequences

Frequent practice of yoga postures will help keep us in good health and good spirits, but it is also easy to apply the basic principles of the yoga poses, breathing and meditation to our everyday lives. If we take time each day to tune into our breath and set aside time to notice how our body, mind and heart feel we will become more in tune with ourselves. In this way we'll recognize when we are beginning to feel off balance and be able to address things and stop the slide.

When feeling under stress or pressure, slow down and breathe steadily and deeply, helping the body and brain to receive more oxygen, allowing the body to become calm and the mind clear. When walking, allow the spine to lengthen and the shoulders relax. If waiting in a queue, gently lift the abdomen and drop the weight evenly into the feet. Whilst watching TV, try sitting in Cobbler Pose (page 45) or cross-legged in Happy Pose (page 38) with the back straight. Always eat slowly. If experiencing difficulties sleeping, practise relaxing the whole body and mind in Corpse Pose (page 65) before going to bed.

Taking refuge in our practice will help create balance in our minds and bodies, bring fresh perspective to our thoughts and feelings, and allow yoga to reach into our lives.

Yoga Sequence for Back Alignment

Backache is probably one of the most common ailments today and is closely linked to stress and tension. It is for this reason that virtually everybody at some point in their lifetime will experience back pain or discomfort. Other contributing factors to back pain are weak abdominal muscles, being overweight and leading a sedentary lifestyle. These all cause poor posture and carriage of the spine which leads to compression of the vertebra, pinching of the nerves and tightness, imbalance and deterioration of the back muscles.

Yoga postures are an excellent antidote to back pain and the following sequence is designed to release muscular stiffness, thus freeing up the spine whilst steadily building muscle strength.

1 *Little Boat Twist* (pages 48-49)

2 *Downward Facing Dog Pose* (page 31)

3 *Mountain Pose* (page 22)

4 *Standing Forward Bend Pose (Step 3)* (page 30)

9 *Sage's Twist Gentler Variation* (page 51)

10 *Sitting Forward Bend Pose (Gentler Variation)* (page 39)

11 *Sleeping Cobbler Pose* (page 45)

12 *Plough Pose (Gentler Variation)* (page 56)

Before embarking on these exercises, check with your doctor that they are suitable for you. When practising, start with the Gentler Variations for each posture and focus on moving your back slowly, smoothly and gently, breathing space and length into your spine. Always be careful not to push or force your back into the poses. Listen to your body as you do your yoga practice; if you begin to feel any strain or tension, particularly in your back, then release the pose, lie on your back and rest, then move on when you feel ready. Be kind to your body and you will find it responds well; little by little the aches will gradually diminish as your back rediscovers its rightful flexibility and strength.

5 *Triangle Pose* (page 26)

6 *Side Angle Pose (Gentler Variation)* (page 32)

7 *Leg Stretch Pose (Step 1 and 2 only)* (page 35)

8 *Child's Pose* (page 64)

13 *Shoulderstand* (page 57)

14 *Knee Hug Pose (Step 1 and 2 only)* (page 41)

15 *Corpse Pose* (page 65)

16 *Happy Pose* (page 38)

Yoga Sequence for Awakening Energy

Breathing fully whilst practising yoga asanas generates energy within the body, and this dynamic, fluid series of postures is designed as a super booster to start your day. When you practise in the morning the body may still be waking up, so take this sequence slowly in order for your body to fully absorb the restorative benefits of each pose. If you have time,

begin with four to six cycles of The Sun Salutation (pages 24-25) before moving on to the postures shown here, as this will help to warm up your muscles and limber up your body for the practice to come.

When you start the day with a yoga practice, you give yourself a fresh beginning as these poses clear the sleep from your

Start this sequence from the final pose of Sun Salutation (pages 24-25).

1 *Triangle Pose* (page 26)

2 *Side Angle Pose* (page 32)

3 *Warrior 1 Pose* (page 28)

4 *Leg Stretch Pose* (page 35)

9 *Sitting Forward Bend Pose* (page 39)

10 *Sleeping Cobbler Pose* (page 45)

11 *Seated Angle Pose* (pages 46-47)

12 *Shoulderstand* (page 57)

head, especially Leg Stretch Pose (page 35) and Headstand (pages 60-61); stimulate your circulation and respiration, see Side Angle Pose (page 32), Camel Pose (page 55) and Shoulderstand (page 57); and awaken your whole system ready for the new day ahead. As you flow smoothly in and out of each asana keep your breath steady and see your breath as light filling your entire body with energy and space. Visualize the light flowing into your body and then out again as you exhale. At first, take five breaths in each pose then gradually, over time, your stamina will develop and you can increase the number of breaths and duration of each pose as your body becomes stronger and your mind sharper.

5 *Cow Face Pose* (page 44)

6 *Camel Pose* (page 55)

7 *Cobra Pose* (page 53)

8 *Half Twisting Fish* (page 50)

13 *Plough Pose* (page 56)

14 *Fish Pose* (page 59)

15 *Headstand* (pages 60-61)

16 *Yoga Sealing Pose* (page 64)

Yoga Sequence for Tension Release

Although this yoga sequence is an ideal wind down from a busy or stressful day, it can also be practised any time to calm the mind and release tension from your muscular and nervous systems.

The neck and shoulders are extremely prone to tension build-up so, as you practise these postures, be conscious of relaxing and releasing these areas each time you breathe out, especially in the Standing Forward Bend Pose (page 30), Sitting Forward Bend Pose (page 39), Eagle Pose (page 37) and the Leg Stretch Pose (page 35).

When you finally come to rest in Corpse Pose (page 65) use a blanket or extra clothes to keep warm then slowly move your

1 *Child's Pose*
(page 64)

2 *Downward Facing Dog Pose*
(page 31)

3 *Standing Forward Bend Pose*
(page 30)

4 *Upward Mountain Pose*
(page 23)

9 *Bridge Building Pose*
(page 54)

10 *Little Boat Twist*
(pages 48-49)

11 *Sitting Forward Bend Pose*
(page 39)

12 *Knee Head Pose*
(page 40)

awareness through your body, starting with your toes and allowing them to completely relax. Work your way slowly up your body consciously relaxing each part as you come to it. From your toes move to your feet and ankles: feel them become heavy as you release the muscles in that area, relax and let go. Continue up your shins, calves, knees and thighs.

Then relax your hips, buttocks, belly, torso, chest and shoulders. Move down your arms relaxing both of your hands and all your fingers then bring your attention to your neck, throat, jaw, mouth, lips, cheeks, eyes and finally even your skin. Feel every inch of your body relaxing, releasing and breathing out tension, anxiety and tiredness.

5 *Tree Pose*
(page 34)

6 *Eagle Pose*
(page 37)

7 *Leg Stretch Pose*
(Stronger Variation)
(page 35)

8 *Side Extension Pose*
(page 33)

13 *Shoulderstand*
(page 57)

14 *Plough Pose*
(Gentler Variation)
(page 56)

15 *Sleeping Cobbler Pose*
(page 45)

16 *Corpse Pose*
(page 65)

Index

Acknowledgments

PUBLISHER'S ACKNOWLEDGMENTS

With thanks to the following companies who supplied clothing and equipment for photography:

Hugger Mugger: yoga mats and props shown throughout the book and on page 17; yoga clothing (yogatard) pages 28-9, 44-45, 53, 58

For details see
www.huggermugger.com

Debbie Moore for Pineapple: leggings on pages 6, 18, 62, 70; yoga outfit on pages 21 (Forward Bend), 30-31, 36-37 and small photos on cover.

6a, Langley Street, London WC2 9JA
Tel: +44 (0)207 836 4006

Freed of London Ltd: pages 20-27, 38-39, 41, 43, 46-47, 56-57, 60-61, 64-65, 68-69 and Jean Hall's outfit on cover.

94, St Martins Lane, London WC2 4AT
Tel: +44 (0)207 240 0432

All other outfits belong to the models.

AUTHOR'S ACKNOWLEDGMENTS

With thanks to John and Val as always, and to all my sisters, blood and otherwise!
Thanks also to Louise Taylor, Alan Kelly, Graham Atkins Hughes, Liberty Shaw and Anya Evans.

PICTURE CREDITS

Bridgeman Art Library: pages 8, 9
Getty Images: pages 10, 11, 12, 13, 14, 15, 22-23, 24-25
ImageState Ltd: page 16